CLASSICAL SOLOS
FOR
FLUTE
VOLUME 2

ONLINE MEDIA INCLUDED
Audio Recordings
Printable Piano Accompaniments

PLAYBACK+
Speed • Pitch • Balance • Loop

T0083358

To access recordings and PDF accompaniments, visit:
www.halleonard.com/mylibrary

Enter Code
5067-7048-1293-4748

ISBN 978-1-70516-748-9

Copyright © 2014 by HAL LEONARD CORPORATION
International Copyright Secured   All Rights Reserved

For all works contained herein:
Unauthorized copying, arranging, adapting, recording, Internet posting, public performance,
or other distribution of the printed or recorded music in this publication is an infringement of copyright.
Infringers are liable under the law.

Visit Hal Leonard Online at
www.halleonard.com

World headquarters, contact:
Hal Leonard
7777 West Bluemound Road
Milwaukee, WI 53213
Email: info@halleonard.com

In Europe, contact:
Hal Leonard Europe Limited
1 Red Place
London, W1K 6PL
Email: info@halleonardeurope.com

In Australia, contact:
Hal Leonard Australia Pty. Ltd.
4 Lentara Court
Cheltenham, Victoria, 3192 Australia
Email: info@halleonard.com.au

LARGO
from *Xerxes*

FLUTE

GEORGE FRIDERIC HANDEL
Arranged by PHILIP SPARKE

Largo (♩ = 68)

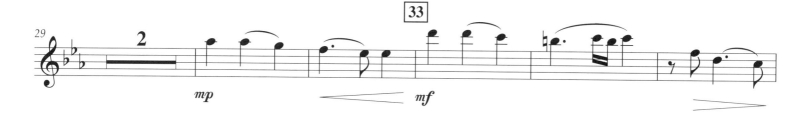

Slower

Copyright © 2014 by Hal Leonard Corporation
International Copyright Secured   All Rights Reserved

SONGS MY MOTHER TAUGHT ME

from *Gypsy Songs*

ANTONÍN DVOŘÁK
Arranged by PHILIP SPARKE

Flute

Copyright © 2014 by Hal Leonard Corporation
International Copyright Secured   All Rights Reserved

00870101

MINUET NO. 2
from *Notebook for Anna Magdalena Bach*

FLUTE

Attributed to CHRISTIAN PEZOLD
Arranged by PHILIP SPARKE

00870101

Copyright © 2014 by Hal Leonard Corporation
International Copyright Secured   All Rights Reserved

LA CINQUANTAINE

from *Two Pieces for Cello and Piano*

JEAN GABRIEL-MARIE
Arranged by PHILIP SPARKE

Copyright © 2014 by Hal Leonard Corporation
International Copyright Secured   All Rights Reserved

00870101

SEE, THE CONQUERING HERO COMES

from *Judas Maccabeus*

GEORGE FRIDERIC HANDEL
Arranged by PHILIP SPARKE

FLUTE

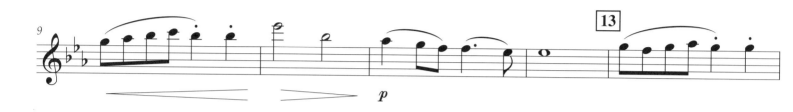

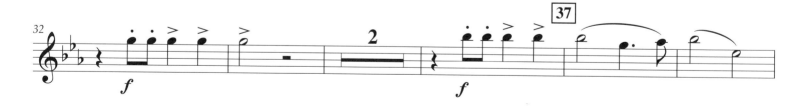

rall.

00870101

Copyright © 2014 by Hal Leonard Corporation
International Copyright Secured   All Rights Reserved

SONATINA
Op. 36, No. 1

MUZIO CLEMENTI
Arranged by PHILIP SPARKE

FLUTE

Copyright © 2014 by Hal Leonard Corporation
International Copyright Secured   All Rights Reserved

SERENATA
from *String Quartet, Op. 3, No. 5*

FRANZ JOSEPH HAYDN
Arranged by PHILIP SPARKE

Flute

Copyright © 2014 by Hal Leonard Corporation
International Copyright Secured   All Rights Reserved

00870101

TAMBOURIN
from *Second Suite in E Minor*

JEAN-PHILIPPE RAMEAU
Arranged by PHILIP SPARKE

FLUTE

Copyright © 2014 by Hal Leonard Corporation
International Copyright Secured   All Rights Reserved

WALTZ
from *Album for the Young*

Flute

PYOTR ILYICH TCHAIKOVSKY
Arranged by PHILIP SPARKE

Copyright © 2014 by Hal Leonard Corporation
International Copyright Secured   All Rights Reserved

00870101

SONATINA
from *Six Pieces, Op. 3*

CARL MARIA VON WEBER
Arranged by PHILIP SPARKE

FLUTE

Moderato e con amore
(♩ = 120)

Copyright © 2014 by Hal Leonard Corporation
International Copyright Secured   All Rights Reserved

00870101

GAVOTTE
from *Paride ed Elena*

CHRISTOPH GLUCK/arr. JOHANNES BRAHMS
Arranged by PHILIP SPARKE

FLUTE

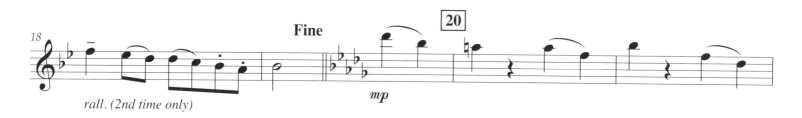

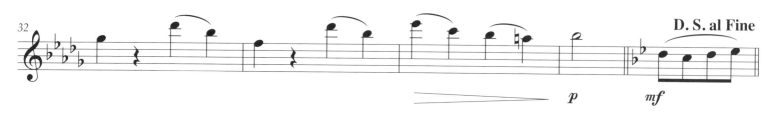

00870101

Copyright © 2014 by Hal Leonard Corporation
International Copyright Secured   All Rights Reserved

SONATA
Op. 118, No. 1

ROBERT SCHUMANN
Arranged by PHILIP SPARKE

FLUTE

Copyright © 2014 by Hal Leonard Corporation
International Copyright Secured   All Rights Reserved

SERENADE
from *Schwanengesang, D.957*

FRANZ SCHUBERT
Arranged by PHILIP SPARKE

FLUTE

00870101

Copyright © 2014 by Hal Leonard Corporation
International Copyright Secured   All Rights Reserved

SONATINA
Anh. 5, No. 1

LUDWIG VAN BEETHOVEN
Arranged by PHILIP SPARKE

Flute

Moderato (♩ = 126)

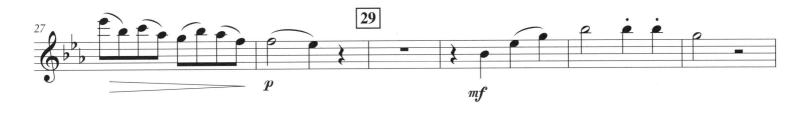

Copyright © 2014 by Hal Leonard Corporation
International Copyright Secured   All Rights Reserved

BOURRÉE
from *Flute Sonata, HWV 363b*

FLUTE

GEORGE FRIDERIC HANDEL
Arranged by PHILIP SPARKE

Copyright © 2014 by Hal Leonard Corporation
International Copyright Secured   All Rights Reserved